Healthy Plates

EATING HEALTHY

VALERIE BODDEN

Published by Creative Education and Creative Paperbacks | P.O. Box 227, Mankato, Minnesota 56002
Creative Education and Creative Paperbacks are imprints of The Creative Company
www.thecreativecompany.us

Design and production by Liddy Walseth | Printed in the United States of America

Photographs by Corbis (Roman Märzinger/Westend61, Maximilian Stock Ltd/the food passionates, Ocean, Scott Phillips/Taunton Press, Lew Robertson, Topic Photo Agency, Chris Whitehead/cultura, Zero Creatives/cultura), Dreamstime (Yen Hung Lin), Getty Images (Kyu Oh), iStockphoto (joeblanger, NormaZaro), Shutterstock (Andrey_Kuzmin, Michel Borges, Pavel Hlystov, Nastya22, victoriaKh)

Library of Congress Cataloging-in-Publication Data
Bodden, Valerie. | Eating healthy / Valerie Bodden. | p. cm. — (Healthy plates) | Summary: An early reader's introduction to the connections between healthy eating and being healthy, benefits of food groups such as vegetables, nutritional concepts such as energy, and recipe instructions. | Includes bibliographical references and index. | ISBN 978-1-60818-507-8 (hardcover) ISBN 978-1-62832-107-4 (pbk) | 1. Nutrition—Juvenile literature. I. Title.
QP141.B635 2015 | 613.2—dc23 | 2014000706

CCSS: RI.1.1, 2, 4, 5, 6, 7; RI.2.2, 5, 6, 7, 10; RI.3.1, 5, 7, 8; RF.1.1, 3, 4; RF.2.3, 4

First Edition 9 8 7 6 5 4 3 2 1

TABLE OF CONTENTS

Healthy Foods

Your body needs food to give it energy and help it grow. But not all foods are good for you. Healthy foods contain the **nutrients** (*NOO-tree-unts*) your body needs to grow and be healthy. Healthy foods are put into five food groups.

HEALTHY FOODS COME IN ALL SHAPES, COLORS, AND SIZES.

Groups of Foods

The dairy food group includes milk and foods made from milk. Dairy foods give your body a nutrient called calcium. Calcium helps make your bones strong. Dairy foods also have protein. Protein helps you grow.

EATING HEALTHY FOODS CAN GIVE YOU MORE ENERGY TO PLAY AND CLIMB.

Bread and cereal are part of the **grain** group. Foods in the grain group have carbohydrates (*kar-bo-HI-drates*). Carbohydrates give your body energy.

PASTA, CRACKERS, BREADS, RICE, AND POTATOES ALL HAVE CARBOHYDRATES.

9

Foods in the fruit group have lots of **vitamins**. Fruits like kiwis and oranges have Vitamin C. Vitamin C heals cuts and helps your body fight **germs**. Your body gets Vitamin A from yellow or orange fruits like peaches. That vitamin gives you good eyesight. Many fruits also have fiber. Fiber helps your **digestive system**.

KIWIS, PINEAPPLE, ORANGES, AND APPLES ARE COLORFUL MEMBERS OF THE FRUIT GROUP.

Vegetables have fiber and vitamins, too. Potatoes and spinach have a nutrient called potassium. Potassium is good for your heart because it keeps your **blood pressure** low.

PLANTS THAT ARE USED FOR FOOD ARE CALLED VEGETABLES.

Meats, nuts, eggs, and beans belong to the protein group. These foods have lots of protein to help your body grow. Foods in the protein group also have vitamins. Meats have a nutrient called iron. Iron helps your blood carry **oxygen** through your body.

DAIRY FOODS LIKE CHEESE AND VEGETABLES LIKE MUSHROOMS ALSO HAVE PROTEIN.

Why Eat Healthy?

Healthy foods can help your body stay strong as you get older. Healthy foods give you energy and help you keep a healthy body weight. Eating healthy foods can even make it easier to pay attention at school.

IF YOU TAKE LUNCH TO SCHOOL, TRY TO PACK A LOT OF FRUITS AND VEGGIES.

Bits of Everything

You should eat foods from each food group every day, if you can. Snack on healthy fruits and vegetables. Eat unhealthy foods such as chips, cookies, and candy only once in a while.

RUNNING AND WALKING
ARE GOOD FORMS OF
EXERCISE YOU CAN DO
EVERY DAY.

Add Exercise

Your body needs exercise to stay healthy, too. You can run, play basketball, or ride your bike. When you are done exercising, you can fill your plate with healthy foods!

MAKE A HEALTHY SNACK:

HAM ROLL-UP

1 TORTILLA

1 SLICE HAM

1 SLICE CHEESE

3 THIN SLICES CUCUMBER

1 THIN SLICE TOMATO

Place your tortilla on a plate. Top with the ham, cheese, cucumber, and tomato. Roll it up, and enjoy your snack. Try to figure out how many food groups you are eating!

GLOSSARY

blood pressure—how hard a person's blood pushes against the blood vessels, or tubes that carry blood through the body

digestive system—the parts of your body used in breaking down food and getting rid of waste

germs—tiny living things that can cause sicknesses in people

grain—the part of some kinds of grasses, such as wheat or oats, that is used to make bread and other foods

nutrients—the parts of food that your body uses to make energy, grow, and stay healthy

oxygen—a gas, or type of air, that people need to breathe

vitamins—nutrients found in foods that are needed to keep your body healthy and working well

READ MORE

Green, Emily K. *Healthy Eating.* Minneapolis: Bellwether Media, 2007.

Head, Honor. *Healthy Eating.* Mankato, Minn.: Sea-to-Sea, 2013.

Llewellyn, Claire. *Healthy Eating.* Laguna Hills, Calif.: QEB, 2006.

WEBSITES

My Plate Kids' Place
http://www.choosemyplate.gov/kids/index.html
Check out games, activities, and recipes about eating healthy.

PBS Kids: Healthy Eating Games
http://pbskids.org/games/healthyeating.html
Play games that help you learn about healthy foods.

Note: Every effort has been made to ensure that the websites listed above are suitable for children, that they have educational value, and that they contain no inappropriate material. However, because of the nature of the Internet, it is impossible to guarantee that these sites will remain active indefinitely or that their contents will not be altered.

INDEX